Never Confuse a Memo with Reality

Never Confuse a Memo with Reality

· · · · · · · · · · · · ·

And Other Business Lessons Too Simple Not to Know

RICHARD A. MORAN

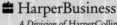

HarperBusiness
A Division of HarperCollins*Publishers*

HarperCollins books may be purchased for educational, business, or sales promotional use. For information please write: Special Markets Department, HarperCollins Publishers, Inc., 10 East 53rd Street, New York, NY 10022.

FIRST EDITION

Designed by Brian Mulligan

Library of Congress Cataloging-in-Publication Data

  Moran, Richard A.
  Never confuse a memo with reality : and other business lessons
too simple not to know / Richard A. Moran. — 1st ed.
    p. cm.
ISBN 0-88730-669-1 (pbk.)
1. Business—Quotations, maxims, etc. I. Title.
HF5351.M825 1994
650—dc20   93-14376

---

93 94 95 96 97 ❖/HC 10 9 8 7 6 5 4 3 2 1

To Brady, Scott, Megan, John,
and everyone else's children

Acknowledgments

Most observations that made it to the pages of this book were learned from other people's mistakes, even though most blunders went unnoticed by the offenders. To them I am most indebted.

To my true co-observers, I appreciate their blinks, winks, courtesies, sighs, stunned silences, and giggles. Key among them is George Bailey, who contributed much to the content of this book and is a real friend. Thanks also to Alan Schnur and my many other colleagues in consulting who can listen fast; to Wilford Butler, my first and best professional mentor; and to Frank Mount, my observant editor.

Finally, much gratitude to John and Louise, my parents, for teaching common sense and to Carol, my wife, for knowing what's important and what's not.

Introduction

In working as an organization change consultant for companies all over the world, I have learned that there are some basic "rules" or organizational behaviors that are too simple not to know.

The observations outlined in this book were not derived through the rigorous application of conjoint analysis in a JIT environment with the Black-Scholes methodology as a denominator. Rather, they are based on the simple organizational truths I find people should know—but don't. I hope this book bridges that gap in the knowledge frontier and makes you more successful.

Rich Moran

Never
Confuse a Memo
with Reality

1. Always know who your client
   or customer is—no matter
   what your job is.

2. Be nice to receptionists—they can help you. If they don't like you, they can hurt you.

3. Never let your guard down around superiors— even when traveling or socializing.

4. Brag about someone to another person; that someone is bound to find out.

5. Simplify, don't complicate—especially processes, procedures, and policies.

6. Never take a problem to your boss without some solutions. You are getting paid to think, not to whine.

7. Spend five minutes figuring out how to communicate the decision for every ten minutes you spend deciding.

8. Believe that change can happen, even after overwhelming evidence says things never seem to get better.

9. Life in business is made up of ambiguous victories and nebulous defeats—claim them all as victories.

10. Know what shoes to wear and keep them in proper shape.

11. When waiting in a lobby for a meeting, or to meet someone, don't sit down.

12. Carry telephone numbers with you—use the back of your calendar or an electronic gadget.

13. Keep track of what you do—someone is sure to ask.

14. Read the business and trade publications—especially *Business Week, Fortune,* and the *Wall Street Journal*—so you understand trends and know buzz words.

15. Don't promise what you can't deliver.

16. Get into the office early.

17. Don't write memos of more than one page, and use graphics where you can.

18. Never miss deadlines.
Ever.

19. Don't be late for meetings. If you are late, don't make it a big deal, just apologize.

20. Always have documents proofread. Never send a document with a typo.

21. When you hear words like "restructuring," "de-layering," and/or "rightsizing," get your résumé together.

22. Be prepared for performance reviews—do your own review in advance and give it to your boss.

23. Get to know the people in the public relations department.

24. If you interview for another job, inside or outside the company, expect that your boss will find out; be prepared.

25. Never confuse a memo with reality . . . most memos from the top are political fantasy.

26. Get out of the office as much as you can—
    especially if you're with clients or customers.

27. Don't look at change as bad.

28. Resignation letters should only be one or two
    lines. Don't take parting shots.

29. Don't tell off-color jokes.

30. Don't take the newspaper to the bathroom.

31. Share the credit for successful projects and make sure everyone's supervisor knows of everyone's contribution.

32. Remember that the purpose of business is to make or do something and sell it. The closer you can get to those activities, the better.

33. If you're in a staff job, get line experience by jumping at assignments out in the trenches.

34. If you tell a racist joke, be
prepared to be fired.

35. As Henry Ford II said, "Never complain, never explain." Be courageous in your business perspectives.

36. Never go into a meeting without your calendar.

37. Focus on the most important things to do to help your department or organization be successful. Don't focus on the easiest things.

38. Never start out a meeting with anything remotely resembling "I'm sorry, I have a cold," or ". . . that we're late," or ". . . there's a typo."

39. Take a time-management course and then develop your own system that will work.

40. As tedious as it may be, understand your health benefits and keep track of them.

41. Collect business cards and keep them in a Rolodex. If you don't think you'll remember how you know the person, make a note on the card.

42. Maintain an accurate mailing list for announcements, newsletters, and sales calls.

43. Go to the company holiday party.

44. Don't get drunk at the company holiday party.

45. Treat your time as if someone is paying for it—someone is.

46. Keep track of expenses or you'll end up losing money.

47. Always carry your business cards with you and give them out freely.

48. Maintain a sense of humor and inject it when appropriate.

49. Return calls within twenty-four hours. Never leave one unanswered.

50. If you're going to complain about something, have a solution in mind and make clear what you want.

51. Develop friends in the executive search-and-placement business.

52. Buy clothes that will last a long time—lean toward wools and cottons.

53. If traveling on the corporate jet, know what the seating protocols are before you get on.

54. Learn to read financial statements.

55. Know how to write business letters and send them—including thank-you letters and proposal letters.

56. In all sales situations seek clarity—is it sold or isn't it?

57. Develop a high tolerance for ambiguity—you'll be more satisfied.

58. Learn to remember people's names. If your memory is poor, develop a system.

59. At all costs, avoid dotted-line or ambiguous reporting relationships.

60. Always have an agenda.

61. Don't hang your diplomas in your office unless you're an M.D.

62. Learn how to give first-rate presentations so that the message you're trying to deliver is the same one the audience receives.

63. Be comfortable around senior managers, or learn to fake it.

64. Don't micromanage your people, your projects, or your own life.

65. If you even *think* you're vulnerable, you should probably find another job.

66. Read *In Search of Excellence*—the companies are dated, but the principles are not.

67. Understand the skills and abilities that differentiate you from everyone else. Whenever you have the opportunity, use them.

68. Learn how to use a spreadsheet software program.

69. Keep a toothbrush and toothpaste in your desk and use them after lunch.

70. Long hours don't mean anything—results count, not effort.

71. Happy workers don't always make good workers, but good workers make for happy workers. . . . Focus your efforts on getting yourself and others to work well.

72. Maintain outside interests—volunteer in not-for-profits and stay physically fit.

73. Write down ideas—they get lost like good pens.

74. Worry more about implementation than strategy—it's harder to do.

75. Learn how to run a meeting well, and learn how to prepare a good meeting agenda.

76. Rejoice in the successful completion of projects and major activities. Remember how it felt to put that calculus text away, knowing you'd never have to open it again.

77. Understand the core of the business and bond with it. Don't take a job at Nintendo if you hate video games.

78. Know the perceptions people have of you. If people see you as "a whiner" or "too political," change that perception.

79. Develop a point of view about success—your own and your organization's.

80. The buzz words from Total Quality Management
are here to stay (for a while). Know what
Continuous Process Improvement and
six sigma mean.

81. Own stock in the company for which you work,
but make sure not all the stock you own
is in one company.

82. Seek rotational assignments, especially if one will put you in a key operational role or close to the seat of power in corporate headquarters.

83. Read *What Color Is Your Parachute?* every year.

84. The true test of whether you (and your company) are customer-driven is how you set priorities. If the question How will this affect customers? is always the first one asked, the chances are good the organization is customer-driven.

85. Never in your life say,

"It's not my job."

86. Read your job description but never be restricted by it. Do what needs to be done.

87. Maintain a three-year rolling career plan.

88. Be known as someone who enhances customer service.

89. When working on the computer, save the document you're working on frequently.

90. If someone says you're not strategic, try to figure out what that means and then tell him or her to go to hell.

91. Don't ever ask colleagues if they dye their hair. Don't ever tell them that they are fat or bald— or that they look tired.

92. If your desk faces the door, don't look up every time someone passes.

93. Take vacations and long weekends. Never let vacation time expire.

94. Strive to be known as a: • Rainmaker
   • People Developer • Decision Maker.

95. Go only to those training classes that will help
   you. Avoid those that will be a waste of time.
   Good training classes will expose you to new
   and exciting ideas.

96. When giving a talk or a presentation, always
   consider what thought you want the audience
   to walk away with.

97. Don't eat garlic at lunch.

98. Relationships change. Your one-time allies can become your nemeses. Remember who is who.

99. Learn how to make proper introductions and then introduce people properly.

100. Always know how you perform—be honest with yourself and do better next time.

101. Always have an answer to the question, What would I do if I lost my job tomorrow?

102. Use a spiral-bound notebook to take meeting notes and record phone-mail messages. It will become your business journal.

103. Maintain a sense of adventure—there are things to do if your travels take you to Erie, Ohio, in February.

104. Get at least one article published per year that will garner recognition in your field.

105. Create a great opening to speeches and presentations—use it often or until you get sick of it.

106. Complete surveys and return them.

107. Don't open any envelope or read any memo marked CONFIDENTIAL unless it's addressed to you.

108. A little self-effacing humor can be an effective icebreaker; just don't use too much.

109. Never assume you can keep major changes a big secret, because you can't. Employees always know.

1 1 0. If you're in a focus group, make sure you can trust everyone before you speak your mind.

1 1 1. When the note on the refrigerator says it will be emptied this Friday, get your salad dressing. Cleaning the refrigerator is the one corporate initiative that's *always* fully implemented.

1 1 2. If you don't know the answer, say so.

113. Reorganizations mean someone will lose his or her job. Get on the task force that will make the recommendations.

114. If you're worried about your job, you probably should be.

115. If everyone else is telling you to worry about your job, you probably should.

116. If you're feeling sorry for yourself, do something, like delivering meals to the homebound, that will snap you out of it.

117. Take a counseling course and develop a "bedside manner" for dealing with clients and associates.

118. Don't take sick days unless you are.

119. Help other people network for jobs—what goes around comes around.

120. Recognizing someone else's contribution will repay you doubly.

121. Know what your pay grade is—what the salary range is, where you are in the range, and how to get to the next level.

122. If you're in a job where someone ever tells you to look busy, look for another job.

123. Do your homework before interviews—reading annual reports, which are easy to get, is the minimum.

124. Give presentations that tell stories, not just provide data.

125. Never put more than twenty words on an overhead slide. Use graphics. If you want to lose the audience, show slides with columns of numbers.

126. Make time for life outside of work.

127. Buy good luggage and briefcases—people notice.

128. Assume no one can/will keep a secret.

129. Make sure you can operate the fax machine, photocopy machine, and report-binding equipment.

130. Never appear stressed in front of a client, a customer, or your boss. Take a deep breath and ask yourself, In the course of human events, how important is this?

131. Never go into a meeting without knowing what you want the outcome(s) to be.

132. If anticipating your first day of work doesn't stir feelings of excitement in your gut, it isn't the right job for you. Don't find out the hard way.

133. Don't check your luggage, and take only the essentials with you. Travel light.

134. Always keep your passport and airline tickets in the same pocket of your suit or briefcase.

135. Spend your department's budget as if it were your own.

136. The days of the three-martini lunch are over—
don't drink at lunch unless you don't plan
to go back to work.

137. No matter what you're told, a laptop
computer will run on the battery for
an hour and a half, max.

138. At most, only half the time you spend on a plane
will be productive: plan accordingly.

139. You're never too old to change, learn a new job, start over, or try something new.

140. Take evening and extension courses.

141. When interviewing, think about the people with whom you'd be working. Eight hours a day is a long time to spend with people you don't enjoy.

142. Life is choices: always choose to do what you will remember ten years from now.

143. Become proficient in another language—or at least get the tapes and try.

144. Make a "to do" list every day. Crossing things off the list is very satisfying.

145. Don't try to be close friends with subordinates.

146. Leave concise phone-mail messages. If you know it will be long, say how many topics you'll cover early in the message.

147. Never leave misspellings in any document that leaves your office—including e-mail.

148. The final presentation/recommendations should never come as a surprise to the client, task force, or your boss.

149. Leave your office building at least once every day, even if it's January and you work in Anchorage. It will clear your head.

150. Never go to more than two meetings a day or you will never get anything done.

151. Befriend your travel agent, and don't be
afraid to demand service.

152. Never correct a co-worker in front of a customer
or client . . . or anyone else.

153. Cooperate with consultants—their input
can change your life.

154. Don't date co-workers.

155. Don't tell people their ideas are bad unless you've got a better one.

156. Commuting is not necessarily bad—you just need a good reason for it, such as loving your job or loving your house. The longer the commute, the better the reason needs to be.

157. Never apologize for an idea that didn't work—but always admit a mistake.

158. Make friends with the guard in the lobby—
someday you will forget your i.d. badge.

159. Be realistic about how much work you can
accomplish at night or on a trip and only pack
that much. Don't overpack your briefcase and
lug too much around.

160. Don't talk about your boss, clients, or projects
in elevators or taxis.

161. Always push that little button that sends callers directly to your phone mail when you are not around. No one likes to wait six rings and then get a recording.

162. Go through an Outward Bound course.

163. Let things go. If the old way doesn't work— don't keep it.

164. You will never regret
having spent too much
time with your kids.

165. Never make up an acronym; try not to use them.

166. Use commuting time well. Listen to National Public Radio, tapes you enjoy, or, if you can afford it, use a car phone to get things done. If using public transportation, read, do paperwork, or get mentally prepared for the day, but don't use a cellular phone.

167. Take risks with your ideas and with implementing them.

168. Use metaphors to convey your point.

169. Be the first to use technology—don't fight it. People talk about the Luddites, but they're history.

170. People who don't know how to use phone mail and personal computers will tend to slow things down—surround yourself with early adapters.

171. Being good is important;

being trusted is essential.

172. Have lunch once a month with someone outside the company who someday might hire you.

173. Become known for building ideas, not for finding fault.

174. Always strive for a deeper level of truth with business associates. Posturing and pretending is always transparent to everyone.

175. Italian salad dressing stains silk ties and blouses and is best avoided.

176. Although everyone hates it, understand the budgeting process and what it means to your group.

177. Learn the difference between Theory X and Theory Y and Type A and Type B and the definition of the Hawthorne Effect.

178. Don't be afraid to ask the big question; other people are probably wondering about it, too.

179. Suggestion systems can work—don't be reluctant to use them.

180. Pick your friends carefully. The water cooler set may be accessible, but those who are there all the time will always be there.

181. Reduce all analysis to three bullet points: no one will take time to understand, pay attention to, or remember any more.

182. Don't have anyone on your team who you wouldn't trust with your kids.

183. When you get the entrepreneurial urge, go visit someone who's started a business—it may cure you.

184. Whenever executives start talking about competition, be prepared for cost reduction.

185. Do something good
early in your new
job or assignment.

186. Never be the last to leave a company going downhill: your personal market value declines each additional day you stay.

187. Cultivate a reputation for being reliable and hardworking, even if it means bucking peer pressure.

188. If you have bad handwriting, buy a laptop and learn word processing. If you have good handwriting, do the same.

189. Strive to be an "impact player," i.e., someone who makes a difference no matter what the situation.

190. Always arrive at work thirty minutes before your boss.

191. Like they say in boxing, "Always finish stronger than you start." People remember the end of the project.

192. You can have fun nearly every day if you approach work with the right attitude.

193. Always plan your day while in the shower.

194. If you think people don't know what you are really after, think again.

195. Recognize that people from headquarters, particularly staff, never know what is going on. Ask the workers directly and you will learn a lot more.

196. Fountain pens always leak. Always. They leak more on airplanes.

197. The old model said that managers didn't do anything but "manage"; the new rules say that managers must do.

198. Be sensitive about the language you use, especially gender-specific titles. Know what the organizational norm is regarding titles like "chairman."

199. The size of your office is not as important as the size of your paycheck.

200. Keep your desk clean and you will think better.

201. It is true. Sometimes you'll be on a roll and everything will click; take maximum advantage. When the opposite is true, hold steady and wait it out.

202. Don't talk about your new car or big sailboat with peers or clients.

203. Trust is as important as competence and
more important than affinity.

204. Remember the parable about the captain of the
battleship steaming through the dark night who
proudly insisted that the ship showing the light
dead ahead give way . . . until the "ship"
identified itself as a lighthouse. It works in many
organizational situations.

205. Remember the story of the flood consultant who confidently told Saint Peter that he would tell the assembly of heaven about how he managed the great Johnstown flood of 1988 . . . until he found out that Noah would be in the audience. Balance humility with expertise.

206. Sometimes saying nothing and waiting until the other side makes a move is the best offense. The Japanese have perfected this strategy.

207. Money now is worth more than money later.

208. Manage the paradox of being 100 percent committed to what you are doing while keeping an eye open for other opportunities.

209. Don't surround yourself with people who are like you: strive for difference and diversity.

210. Never wear a tie with a stain on it.

211. Boil down your job far enough so that you can describe it to anyone easily.

212. If Total Quality Management doesn't get some results for your organization in one year, it should be history.

213. Coffee and doughnuts are a meal.

214. If a job sounds too good to be true, it probably is.

215. A good source of names for initiatives and speeches are country-western album covers.

216. Learn what finished work looks like and
     then deliver your own work only when it
     looks the same way.

217. Act like the customer is king, even if no one else
     in your organization does.

218. Develop a network of friends and advisers that
     can give you advice on issues you are dealing
     with. Think of this as your own personal
     board of directors.

219. The most successful people in business are also the most interesting.

220. Avoid being assigned for longer than a year to the human resources department.

221. Learn how to involve people in your work.

222. Be honest with yourself about your strengths and weaknesses and manage accordingly.

223. Stay with something long enough to learn and make a contribution.

224. Bring your kids to the office so they can see where you work.

225. The age of strategic planning is over . . . it is now the age of implementation.

226. Those who do the work
should have a say in how
it's to be organized.

227. It may not be a small world, but there is a small number of people who count.

228. Learn to recognize people who are bad medicine and stay away from them.

229. Whatever initiatives you are communicating, remember to tell your audience three things: What it is and why, how it will affect them, and when they will know more.

230. Always ask why before proceeding.

231. Don't create reports that sit on shelves. Reports should be a means to an operational end.

232. The lifespan of any organization's design is less than twenty-four months. Stay tuned if you don't like what you see.

233. Don't listen to rock and roll in your office.

234. Give informational interviews.

235. Graciousness always helps: when you have a visitor, make sure you offer soft drinks or coffee.

236. Send thank-you notes to people who help you.

237. Don't get a reputation for being a climber or a political animal; get a reputation for always doing what is right.

238. Have your own document retention program: if you haven't referred to a file in twelve months, get rid of it.

239. Being in the right place at the right time is never an accident.

240. Never underestimate the ability of people to develop strange interpretations of anything you write, say, or do.

241. Remember that almost all business is painfully simple. Strive to demystify.

242. Keep the good pens in your desk, otherwise you lose them.

243. The person who spends all of his or her time at work is not hardworking, he or she is boring.

244. Don't confuse extensive documentation of a
      situation with insight, and don't confuse
      spreadsheets with analysis.

245. Most autocratic executives are like the man
      behind the curtain in the Wizard of Oz: they
      are really more human than the wizards they
      are trying to be.

246. Create work teams with the best available talent,
      regardless of function or background.

247. Teamwork will become more and more important. Learn what it is and how to be a good team member.

248. In projects and meetings prepare rigorous lists of things to do with dates—learn to use tools like GANT charts.

249. Watch a big reorganization closely. It will broadcast what will be important in the company. Remember, "same old horses, same old glue."

250. Just because you are in business and have a family doesn't mean you can't be in shape—it actually makes it even more important.

251. Don't get hung up defining whether you're working on a vision or a mission or goals or objectives—do what's important.

252. Know when you are at your best—morning, night, under pressure, relaxed—and schedule and prioritize work accordingly.

253. If you're put in a spot where you are the process consultant, keep the meeting moving and know your audience.

254. Don't create layers.

255. Always have a beginning, middle, and end,
whether it be a presentation, a meeting,
a memo, or a letter.

256. Don't be a process consultant without having
some content knowledge as well.

257. Learn what the differences are between
marketing, sales, public relations,
and advertising.

258. There is a marketing element to everything you do in any organization.

259. Customers don't care how you're organized— they care most about responsiveness, cost, and speed.

260. The best mission statement ever written is that of Federal Express: To deliver the package the very next morning, regardless.

261. Never sacrifice quality to
make numbers.

262. Don't be internally focused. Learn what's important to customers and clients.

263. Every change initiative will have an impact on other parts of the organization; know what the impact might be.

264. Understanding the difference between what the organization says and what it does will help focus on basic problems.

265. Work elimination should accompany job elimination—someone needs to pay attention to the balance, i.e., with job elimination, work elimination should also occur.

266. Work on problems, not symptoms. Morale itself is never a problem; something is happening that causes low morale, which creates a problem.

267. Don't sell anything in the office, except Girl Scout cookies.

268. Work for a company where pay equals performance.

269. The fastest way to create organizational change is to change people.

270. The best thing about training is the people you meet in your class.

271. If you learn and apply even one idea from a training session, it has been worthwhile.

272. The hard part of any process is determining who decides who decides.

273. Never communicate anything important, such as "You're fired" or "I quit" over the car phone or on phone mail.

274. Learn the difference between benchmarking and best practices.

275. Try to figure out who's making decisions.

276. "Playing with the lights" means a lot of activity where nothing will happen.

277. Call home every night
when you're on the road.

278. Beware of a false sense of activity—i.e., you're too busy to go to the bathroom but you're not sure what all of your work will add up to.

279. Action follows intent: if you intend to lose weight, act like you're on a diet. If you intend to be customer- or quality-driven, act that way.

280. If the "answer" to an organizational issue is already declared or known, test the answer before you waste time coming up with a new one.

281.   Most problems can be lumped into three types:
        organizational, process, or cultural. Although
        they are not unrelated, know which is which.
        Understanding the category will help you
        derive solutions.

282.   Before you get retrained for a new job, make
        sure where the retraining will get you and
        that you'll learn something new.

283. Real change in any organization usually happens due to an outside impetus.

284. Read the fine print in early-retirement packages.

285. Try to make your hobbies into a career.

286. Own your own career.

287. Learn the paradoxes of organization work, like growing the organization while maintaining cost controls.

288. Be a supporter of the latest fad, but don't build your career around it.

289. Never travel in first class if your customer and your boss don't, even if you've used a cheap upgrade coupon.

290. Don't try to save money on travel expenses if it means you'll lose a productive minute working on whatever you are traveling for.

291. Don't make people feel
bad when they make
a mistake.

292. Never complain about jet lag.

293. Read the same book the boss is reading.

294. Training is often seen as a reward and a sign that the organization is willing to invest in you. Take advantage of it, but be realistic about what you will really learn.

295. Don't expect that things will be different back at the ranch after you finish a training program.

296. The best training is provided by your customers.

297. Be direct but not confrontational.

298. Never try to accomplish more than three things in any one meeting.

299. Get assigned to a project team working with external consultants. You may learn something and protect your job at the same time.

300. Globalization is really happening.

301. Support recycling. Avoid wasting paper.

302. Learn the definition of outsourcing and find out whether or not you are a target.

303. Drink coffee and drive, or talk on the phone and drive, but don't do all three at once.

304. If you are placed on a Total Quality team, do something worthwhile; don't redesign forms.

305. Always get a title and sufficient money going into a company: promises about future potential are always overstated.

306. There are work clothes, school clothes, and church clothes. Don't mix them up. The focus at work should be the organization, not your socks.

307. Don't expect to make money in the boat or wine business.

308. Performance evaluations
take place every day,
not every six months
or every year.

309. Ask questions at company meetings, but
don't embarrass anyone.

310. Job security does not exist.

311. When giving a presentation, don't read
the slides and don't use a pointer.

312. The concept of entitlement is disappearing fast.
You have to earn employment and benefits.

313. Employees always know what's going on in a company. When making announcements assume no one will be surprised.

314. If you order a drink, name the label you want. Don't just say, "I'll have a scotch."

315. Eliminate guilt: don't cheat on expense reports, taxes, benefits, or your colleagues.

316. Let the business shape the organization, not the organization shape the business.

317. A good raise is 10 percent.

318. FUD is the IBM acronym for an illness called Fear, Uncertainty, and Doubt. If you have it, it will probably last for a while, but fight it any way you can.

319. The organization most of us grew up with is gone. Corporate chaos is here to stay.

320. Always carry a thin, cheap calculator.

321. When traveling internationally, read a simple travel guide in advance and carry a quick reference guide to currency exchange.

322. Technology cannot solve all problems. It only can make the real work cheaper, faster, and less tedious.

323. Reducing costs, increasing compensation, or providing more training are usually not the solutions to organizational problems.

324. Don't work on weekends—
work longer during the
week if you have to.

325. Companies like UPS may not do everything right but they sure keep their trucks clean and their people courteous. There is a lesson in paying attention to details like people and trucks.

326. Don't smoke. Especially don't hang around out front of the building with other smokers.

327. If you receive a customer complaint letter, give him or her what he or she wants.

328. Take a good presentation skills class.

329. If you get a bad review, be sure you understand what genuinely needs to be improved upon, as opposed to your boss's perception of how bad things are.

330. Make decisions in a timely fashion, even if you're not 100 percent certain that it's the right decision. Not deciding is a decision, too.

331. The fewer the policies and procedures, the better.

332. If the result of a meeting is a form, it was a meeting that produced the wrong deliverable.

333. When giving presentations, read the audience continuously. Change the tenor, subject, or speaker if you are losing them.

334. Hanging around in an office lobby will give you a flavor of what it's like to work in the organization.

335. Don't carry huge calendars with all the gizmos and gadgets. They will label you as a staffer.

336. Focus on what peers and supervisors will remember.

337. Preparing budgets and anything related to them is a necessary evil but not a good use of anyone's time or energy.

338. Remember what Stanley Marcus said: "You achieve customer satisfaction when you sell merchandise that doesn't come back to a customer who does."

339. Never pay a relative to fix your car. Never fix your relative's car. The car will always work better if it's taken to the shop. The same holds true for doing taxes, writing résumés, developing business plans, public relations, and all other business functions.

340. Always sit at the conference table—never by the wall.

341. Constructing a matrix can create a very powerful picture. Use one whenever you can.

342. Follow Stephen Covey's suggestion of knowing how to distinguish what's important and what's urgent.

343. Career planning is an oxymoron: the most exciting opportunities tend to be unplanned.

344. Treat everyone in the organization with respect and dignity whether it be the janitor or the president. Don't ever be patronizing.

345. Learn to enjoy the present and don't be too future-oriented. Your life will probably not change dramatically once you move from a Grade 9 to a Grade 11.

346. Past performance is the best indicator of future performance. Remember this whenever a leopard claims to have changed its spots.

347. Be wary of slogans like "The Future Is Here" or "Excellence Through People." Look for the beef.

348. Regardless of his tone and style, Tom Peters is almost always right. Read what he's written.

349. Children are a source of truth and ideas. The icebreaker to use in intense meetings was developed by a six-year-old: "Raise your hand who's mad."

350. Be loyal to your career,
your interests, and
yourself.

351. Don't use the speaker phone unless you're on a conference call.

352. All employees—including the management—want to know three things when they show up for work: What's my job? How am I doing? and, How does my contribution help serve the organization's mission?

353. Learn how to stand up in front of a room and take notes at the same time.

354. If your job isn't going well, change jobs before you even think about taking your frustrations out on your co-workers, your family, or yourself.

355. Always know the answer to the question, "What business are we in?"

356. If you write a customer complaint letter, tell the company what you want.

357. Don't confuse the organization chart with who does what. Real activity often takes place between the organization chart lines.

358. Don't treat people like they are dead if they get fired or laid off.

359. Use the word "paradigm" no more
than once a week.

360. Written visions, missions, and goals are not as
important as knowing what you're supposed to
do when you show up in the morning.

361. When someone tells you these are the best years of your life, believe it and act accordingly. They are.